Original title:
Ripe and Ready

Copyright © 2025 Creative Arts Management OÜ
All rights reserved.

Author: Seraphina Caldwell
ISBN HARDBACK: 978-1-80586-335-9
ISBN PAPERBACK: 978-1-80586-807-1

When Hours Gather

The clock's a jester, tick-tock-tick,
Laughter spills from its little tick.
Seconds slide on banana peels,
Time's a prank that never heals.

Gather 'round, the hours collide,
With giggles and glee, we bide.
Each minute in a silly hat,
A dance party started by a rat!

Serenade of the Mature

In gardens where the tomatoes grin,
A serenade thick as my chin.
Laughing cucumbers dance in rows,
Spinach sings as the lettuce glows.

Carrots jest with a leafy bow,
As veggies chat about the wow.
Their golden days in the sun they share,
A chorus blooms with giddy flair.

Pulse of the Orchard

The apples play a funky tune,
Swinging branches, under the moon.
Pears chuckle, swaying side to side,
With every gust, they take a ride.

A breeze of giggles through the trees,
Blossoms chuckle with the bees.
Nature's heart beats in a whirl,
As fruits twirl 'round in a silly swirl.

Sweet Tang of Potential

A lemon dreams of lemonade,
Basking in the sun's warm shade.
Sour faces turn to glee,
When zestful smiles are wild and free.

Mangoes revel in their sweet tease,
Waiting to dance in summer's breeze.
Juicy whispers of flirty fun,
In potential's embrace, they run.

Fruits of Patience

The apple on the tree, quite bold,
Hides with secrets, stories untold.
It whispers sweet, 'Don't pluck too soon,'
While mocking birds sing, beneath the moon.

Bananas laugh in yellow attire,
Joking 'Take your time, don't rush the fire!'
With peels slipping folks on their way,
They chuckle, 'Patience wins the day!'

Overtures of Growth

A tiny seed in soil does dwell,
While dreaming dreams of a garden swell.
'Just give me time,' it sings with glee,
'You'll see me towering, wait and see!'

A sprout then pokes its head out wide,
With sun and rain as faithful guide.
It giggles, 'Look at me, I'm tall!'
But then trips on roots and starts to sprawl.

Eloquent Deliciousness

In the fridge, a yogurt pines,
With flavors dancing, all divine.
It winks and sighs, 'Oh, I could shine,
But you keep me waiting, oh so fine!'

The cheese sits grinning, cheeky and brash,
'Aged to perfection, just in a flash!'
Yet all alone, it starts to mope,
'Hurry, my friend, or I might lose hope!'

Senses in Overdrive

Tomatoes blushing with vibrant flair,
Chide the peppers 'Dance, if you dare!'
Onions giggle, oh what a smell,
'Chop us up, and ring the dinner bell!'

Garlic whispers, 'I'm the life of a feast!'
While herbs and spices stir for a tease.
'Let's throw a party,' they shout with zest,
'To tantalize taste buds, that's our quest!'

The Waiting Symphony

In the garden, whispers play,
Carrots dance, while cabbages sway.
Radishes tease with their vibrant red,
'We're almost there!' the tomatoes said.

The peas are prancing, feeling fine,
But lettuce is just wasting time.
With every breeze that comes and goes,
The flowers giggle, 'Here comes the show!'

Blossom's Embrace

The flowers laugh, a colorful crew,
'We've grown so much, how about you?'
Sunshine giggles, tickles the air,
While bees buzz around in a fuzzy flare.

Petals flounce in a giggly dance,
Each bloom's a part of nature's prance.
'Grow up fast!' says the wise old tree,
'But don't forget, you're still carefree!'

From Bud to Bloom

A little bud with dreams so bright,
Wonders when it'll take its flight.
'Will I be fresh, or just a tease?'
Pondering life with the buzzing bees.

A sunflower whispers, 'Don't you fret!
In time, you'll be the best one yet!'
With petals wide, and colors bold,
A tale of growth that never gets old.

Time's Savoring

Tick-tock goes the garden clock,
As veggies giggle, in a joyful flock.
'Wait your turn!' shouts the wise old sage,
'It's all about pacing, not the stage!'

Zucchini jokes that it's lost its way,
While peppers plan a fun ballet.
Together they chuckle, in sun-soaked cheer,
'We'll ripen up, but first, let's clear!'

The Joy of Succulence

In the garden, fruits dangle free,
A cheeky pear stares at me.
"Pick me, pick me," it starts to shout,
While others just grin, without a doubt.

Tomatoes blush in a sunny parade,
Waving seeds, mischief well laid.
Cucumbers giggle, stretched out on vines,
Telling each other they're just divine!

Berries bounce with a juicy flair,
Chasing bees, causing quite a scare.
"Catch me if you can!" they tease and run,
Life in the garden is all just fun!

But watch your step on this fruity spree,
A banana peel's lurking, just wait and see!
With laughter and jests, we gather 'round,
The joy of succulence all around.

Feast of Life

Gather 'round for a colorful feast,
Where veggies play like a wild beast.
Carrots do a jig, radishes roll,
Lettuce leaves laugh, that's their goal!

A corn cob whispers, "I'm buttered and bold!"
While potatoes boast of stories retold.
Tomatoes flirt, all dressed in red,
Saying, "We're fabulous, just like bread!"

Onions cry out, "We bring the tears!"
But don't you worry, we'll quell those fears.
With laughter sprouting from every plate,
The feast of life, it's never too late!

So grab your forks, let the fun commence,
Each bite's an adventure, it makes perfect sense.
With veggies and giggles all in one,
Join the party, let's savor the fun!

Juicy Promises

In the garden, fruits collide,
With squishy grapes that laugh and slide.
Tomatoes blush in the sunny glow,
Trying to outshine the beans below.

Carrots dance beneath the dirt,
Wiggling free in a bright green skirt.
Peppers puff up their colorful skin,
Making sure the party's about to begin.

The Season of Plenty

Watermelons roll in slippery glee,
Calling everyone to join the spree.
Cucumbers giggle with a crunching sound,
While onions watch, perplexed, from the ground.

Zucchini dream of being a boat,
While pumpkins boast of their hefty coat.
Berries sing sweet songs in the vine,
All arguing which one is divine.

Luscious Offerings

In the orchard, trees exchange grins,
As squirrels play tag and joy truly begins.
Peaches are blushing with every bite,
Challenging pears to a friendly fight.

Strawberries strut in their juicy red,
Competing for crowns on each leafy head.
Grapefruits chuckle in their zesty game,
While apples declare, 'We're all the same!'

Savoring Nature's Gifts

Nature's buffet is quite a scene,
Where beans are hopping, and corn is seen.
Salads giggle in bowls with dressings,
While forks come dancing, making blessin's.

Bunches of herbs join the lively show,
Spreading their fragrance, causing a glow.
Eating outdoors, beneath the sun's rays,
With food so funny, it brightens our days.

Fulgent Moments

Sunlight snaps, a golden dance,
On cheeks so round, they take a chance.
Juicy joy in every bite,
Laughter bubbles day and night.

Giggling fruits in rows they sit,
Bouncing balls of sweetness, what a hit!
Nature's candy, bright and bold,
Scrumptious tales waiting to unfold.

With messy hands and grins so wide,
Each squishy treasure tossed aside.
An orchard's playground, oh what fun,
Chasing flavors 'til we're done.

So take a seat, join the spree,
In this feast, there's room for three.
A giggle with each delightful taste,
Seconds, thirds, there's no time to waste.

A Feast of Colors

In gardens bright, a rainbow speaks,
Where purple, orange, yellow peaks.
Pineapples wear their crowns with pride,
While carrots dance in orange stride.

A tomato's blush, oh what a sight,
Cucumbers in their jackets tight.
Radishes roll, they're feeling bold,
In this banquet, life unfolds.

Plates piled high, a colorful spree,
With each new bite, wild jubilee.
Veggies giggle, fruits take a bow,
Who knew a meal could cause such wow?

So grab a fork, let's make a mess,
In this realm of taste, no less.
Eating rainbows, what a treat,
A feast of colors, can't be beat!

Gathering the Essence

In a basket, treasures plucked,
Nature's bounty, oh so lucked.
Sweet melodies from trees above,
Whispers of the season's love.

Peaches blush, they wink at me,
Cherries dance on the cherry tree.
Every nibble, a giggly thrill,
Each drop of nectar, heart to fill.

With playful hands, we gather cheer,
Filling jars with laughter near.
Sticky fingers, hilarious plight,
Nature's essence, pure delight.

So come along, let's make a cheer,
For each small fruit, let's raise a beer!
In every jar, a story spun,
Gathering goodies, oh what fun!

Alluring Treasures of the Earth

Tucked in soil, secrets sleep,
Nutty biscuits, sweet and cheap.
Each dig brings giggles, what a sight,
In muddy boots, the day feels right.

Carrots shy, they hide away,
Till playful hands decide to play.
Onions chuckle as they roll,
Making messes, that's the goal.

Pumpkins pop with a wink so sly,
Underneath a blushing sky.
Each treasure found, a funny quest,
A farmer's life, oh what a jest!

Dig deep down for golden fate,
With laughter loud, we just can't wait.
Nature's gifts, a foamy mirth,
In digging joys, we find our worth.

Buffeted by Sweetness

Fruits jiggle like jelly, oh what a sight,
Branches bowed down, heavy with delight.
Bees buzzing, wearing their sweet little hats,
Grapes giggle softly, sharing tales with the spats.

Bananas slip past, in a dance of cheer,
Even the apples are rolling, oh dear!
Watermelons gossip, pretending they're cool,
While pears play chess, acting like fools.

Nature's Lush Embrace

The fields are a buffet, everyone's invited,
Cauliflower dreams, oh how they've delighted.
Spinach is flexing, showing off its greens,
While carrots race by, plotting grand schemes.

Tomatoes are blushing, so ripe and round,
Zucchinis are buzzing, groovin' to sound.
Pumpkins are chuckling, growing so tall,
And cucumbers whisper, planning a ball.

Essence of Fruition

Strawberries are strutting, dressed in bright red,
While cherries are laughing, bumping heads in bed.
Peaches are peachy, with a smile so wide,
As blueberries gossip, with pride they confide.

Plums plop down, just too fabulous to see,
The lemon's sour face, trying to be free.
With passionfruit puns, they roll on the ground,
Laughter in the orchard, spreading joy all around.

Bounty of the Heavens

Clouds burst forth goodies, like candy from space,
Gummy bears raining, what a hilarious chase!
Chocolate rivers flow, with marshmallows afloat,
Kids in their boats, trying hard not to gloat.

Jellybeans dancing, hopping in rows,
Lollipops spinning, giving sweet shows.
Rainstorms of sprinkles, a delicious parade,
As everyone giggles in sugar-soaked shade.

Palette of the Earth

Colors collide, a messy scene,
Nature's canvas, oh what a dream.
Red radishes dance, green beans play,
While pumpkins grumble, 'Give us our day!'

Squirrels wear hats made of sweet corn shells,
While carrots chuckle in their orange bells.
Berries gossip about who's the best,
As the veggies argue, 'Let's just eat the rest!'

Unveiling Sweetness

Bananas giggle in a fruity parade,
Spoiling the apples, 'We've got it made!'
Pineapples strut in a tall, leafy crown,
While grapes slip and slide, nearly fall down!

Cherries blush bright when the peaches tease,
'You've got the sun-kissed vibe, if you please!'
Watermelons roll, with a splash and a grin,
'Step aside, my friends, let the fun begin!'

The Climax of Seasons

Autumn arrives with a swirl and a twirl,
Pumpkins propose a big harvest whirl.
Frosty mornings make cabbages shiver,
While laughter and joy make the whole world quiver.

In winter's breach, sprouts wrap up tight,
Planning a scheme for their springtime flight.
But here comes the sun with a wink and a wave,
'Let's pop out of hibernation, be bold and brave!'

Vibrant Cornucopia

A basket spills over with colors galore,
'We're more than just food, we're fun to explore!'
Pears play tag with the purple plums,
As jolly old oranges hum silly drums.

Radishes tell tales of their spicy delight,
'We all have our quirks, let's party tonight!'
Every morsel a character, bold and unique,
Gather 'round folks, it's time to critique!

Abundant Echoes

In the garden, with much flair,
The vegetables start to stare.
Tomatoes blush a shade of red,
While cucumbers peek from their bed.

Carrots giggle underground,
As they wiggle, making sounds.
Pepper plants toss a funny dance,
Hoping for just one more chance.

Nurtured by Sunlight

Underneath the sun's warm beam,
Lettuce blooms, a leafy dream.
Zucchinis share a silly joke,
While broccoli feels like a bloke.

Radishes play hide and seek,
In their patches, oh so meek.
With every leaf that starts to grow,
They throw a party down below.

Hues of Expectation

Purple eggplants wear a dress,
Green beans flex without a stress.
Squash rolls in, it's quite a scene,
In this colorful cuisine.

As harvest days draw ever near,
The fruits conspire, full of cheer.
With giggles bright, they do declare,
It's time for snacks, if you dare!

The Taste of Anticipation

Berries waiting for a bite,
Making dessert the biggest fright.
Melons whisper tales of sweet,
As they dream of a juicy treat.

Peas in pods begin to cheer,
Singing songs to bring you near.
With each bite, the laughter flows,
In the garden, joy just grows.

Ripened Dreams

Morning light brings laughter,
As fruits begin to play.
Bananas wear a pillow,
Shapeshifting all the day.

Grapes hold a secret party,
Tiny hats, they cheer.
Peaches join the conga line,
No inhibitions here!

Apples slice up punchlines,
Jokes tossed with every bite.
Citrus throws a zest fest,
Juicy humor feels just right.

In this orchard every hour,
Is filled with pure delight.
With laughter dripping sweetly,
Every fruit takes flight.

The Art of Ripening

Pineapples wear sunglasses,
Chillin' in the sun.
Pears are painting pictures,
Of the fun they've spun.

Kiwi's cracking wise jokes,
While hanging on a vine.
Mangoes wrote a song,
About sunshine, oh so fine!

Watermelons split their sides,
Laughter in each seed.
Plums perform their stand-up bits,
And everyone's agreed.

In this fruity gallery,
The art is truly grand.
With humor in abundance,
Let's all lend a hand!

Blossoms of Anticipation

Buds are gossiping softly,
In the garden so alive.
Each bloom is a chatterbox,
Buzzing how they thrive.

Tulips tell a ticklish tale,
Daisies laugh in a row.
Sunflowers wink their petals,
And giggles start to grow.

The daisies play hide and seek,
While vines pretend to dance.
Lilies chase the butterflies,
In a twirl and a prance!

With every color bursting,
In this joyful place,
Nature's got a punchline,
And a smile on its face.

Embracing the Bounty

Harvest is a funny time,
With pumpkins in disguise.
They're rolling in the hay,
Hiding from prying eyes.

Zucchinis are quite clever,
In their sneaky little ways.
They love to pull a prank,
On all those gloomy days.

Rainbow chard is strutting,
With colors bright and bold.
Telling tales of mischief,
In whispers to be told.

So grab a basket, chuckle,
At all the quirky sights.
In this garden of abundance,
Laughing feels so right!

Harvest Moonlight

Beneath the glow of moonlit skies,
The pumpkins dance in their disguise.
They laugh and jig, with glee they prance,
While scarecrows join the harvest dance.

The cornfields sway, they twist and shout,
As squirrels plan a sneaky route.
To snag the corn before it's bare,
A nutty thief with quite the flair.

In the orchard, apples hang so low,
They gossip 'bout the pears in tow.
"Who's sweeter?" they ponder with delight,
While bees buzz by to join the fight.

So grab a basket, don't you fret,
This autumn's bounty is a safe bet.
With funny faces all around,
A harvest party's quite profound!

Fruits of Anticipation

In the garden, seedlings plop,
Tomatoes giggle, never stop.
They hide behind the leafy greens,
Making plans for all their scenes.

The carrots blush, they're deep in ground,
Sneaky radishes all around.
"We're spicy, sure, but look at us!"
They puff their roots with quite a fuss.

Berries burst with joy in rows,
Cherries challenge folks with prose.
They stage a jam, a fruit parade,
And dance to tunes of sweet charade.

So let's indulge, let's taste the fun,
Each juicy bite's a secret won.
With fruits in hand, let's raise a cheer,
Anticipation brings us near!

The Season of Abundance

A basket full, a tumbling spree,
With veggies talking, wild and free.
They boast of size, they strut with pride,
In gardens lush, they won't abide.

The zucchini laughs, it grows the most,
While peppers plan a spicy toast.
"Who needs a grill?" the onions say,
"We'll make this salad steal the day!"

Eggplants plump, in purple coats,
With whispers shared, they cast their votes.
For the best dish that catches fame,
While basil dreams of herbs to claim.

So grab your forks, let's make a feast,
With dishes new, our joy's unleashed.
Abundance reigns in every bite,
A funny twist to every night!

Plump Promises

The strawberries promise bright and bold,
With whispers sweet, their tales unfold.
Each berry laughs, they crown the bush,
In juicy dreams, their flavors rush.

The grapes debate who's best in wine,
While figs make plans for summer's shine.
"I'll sweeten things up, just you wait!"
They chuckle, knowing they're first-rate.

The cherries try their hand at cheer,
A sour face is what they fear.
They holler loud, "Let's have a ball!"
And dice with fate to win it all!

So when you bite, just know it's true,
Each plump promise is made for you.
With giggles shared, we'll feast tonight,
On nature's treats that feel so right!

Nature's Invitation

The trees are dancing, waving leaves,
Squirrels hitching rides on playful eaves.
Flowers giggle in shades of bright,
In this garden, all feels just right.

Bees buzz around like they own the place,
While frogs leap about, a clumsy race.
Ants march in line, a tiny parade,
Nature's a party, and we're all invited!

Clouds are fluffing, a cottony crowd,
With whispers of sunshine, they all seem proud.
Birds chirp loudly, sharing their glee,
In this wild playground, come join, just be!

So grab your hat, let loose your shoes,
Join the fun, there's nothing to lose.
Nature's calling, a humorous call,
Step outside, laugh, and enjoy it all!

Gentle Maturation

Oh, the fruits laugh, on branches they cling,
Making faces and bubbles, they dance and sing.
Tomatoes blush in a curious way,
While peppers strut like they own the day.

Carrots peek out, with tops in a curl,
"Are we vegetables or part of a whirl?"
Broccoli sports its green, fluffy crown,
Feeling quite proud, like a royal gown.

The melons roll, plotting a spree,
Saying, "Let's blend, oh can't you see?"
With comical grace, they stage a show,
In the garden's patch, fun's guaranteed to flow.

So join the jest, don't shy away,
Nature's flowers bloom in bright array.
As time ticks by, laughter will rise,
In this garden of joys, where humor lies!

When Colors Burst

Look at the petals, such splashes of cheer,
Daring each other, "Come closer, my dear!"
Sunflowers boast with smiles so wide,
While daisies giggle, right by their side.

Marigolds tease, dressed up in gold,
With secrets of sunshine, they eagerly hold.
Zinnias wink, like they know what's planned,
A colorful riot, all perfectly grand.

Bumblebees tumble, tripping their flight,
Chasing the colors, what a hilarious sight!
Orchids stand tall, a graceful show,
Swirling and twirling, stealing the glow.

As petals sway, the day takes flight,
Join in the fun, make everything bright!
With laughter and joy, we'll sing along,
In this colorful world, where we all belong!

Overflowing Dreams

A pot of wishes, visions abound,
Bursts of joy, all around.
Pudding pops giggle, drippin' in delight,
As they dream big dreams, oh what a sight!

Cakes waddle by, with layers so high,
Each slice is a story, don't be shy!
Brownies shimmy with a fudgy cheer,
"Dig in, my friends, we've plenty here!"

Jars of jelly dance with a jig,
Spreading their sweetness, oh so big.
Marshmallows float on clouds of a dream,
With laughter and whipped cream, we all beam.

So grab a spoon, let the fun commence,
In the world of treats, it's sheer nonsense.
Overflowing with laughter, happiness swoops,
In this land of flavors, we all group!

From Bud to Bloom

A tiny bud on a frisky vine,
It wobbles like it's had too much wine.
With hopes of sunshine in its sight,
It dreams of being a flower so bright.

But oh! What a clumsy little sprout,
It tripped on a leaf and fell right out.
With petals outstretched, it strikes a pose,
Laughing at the garden's silly woes.

As bees buzz in and neighbors stare,
It plays charades with nary a care.
While giggling flowers dance along,
The bud beams proud, singing its song.

From sprout to bloom, it's quite the play,
In the grand garden, it steals the day.
With petals like confetti, it twirls around,
A comical sight, where fun is found.

Symphony of Sweetness

In the orchard, juicy and bright,
Fruits are jamming, oh what a sight!
An apple sings with a melodic grin,
While bananas clap, ready to begin.

"Let's mash it up!" shouts a bold pear,
With rhythm so catchy, who wouldn't dare?
The berries burst with noting to spare,
Creating a harmony beyond compare.

With cherries flipping like they own the stage,
Each fruit a character, full of rage.
Citrus zingers, they twist and shout,
Don't forget the antics they're all about!

A symphony fruity in the sunny air,
The garden's alive with laughter to share.
Each drop of juice, a note in the mix,
Together they play, a fruity fix!

The Color of Perfection

In the produce aisle, what a parade,
Tomatoes blush in a vibrant charade.
Peppers jive with their colors so bold,
Giggling together, their stories unfold.

A rogue carrot wears a bright, green top,
Boasting its crunch, it just won't stop.
The eggplant chuckles, wearing a grin,
Saying, "I'm here! Let the feast begin!"

The broccoli, proud, strikes a pose so grand,
While zucchinis cater with pots in hand.
Lettuce bounces, feeling oh-so-fine,
In this riot of veggies, all ghoulishly shine.

With hues galore, it's a vivid dance,
Every color leaps, it's a funny romance.
From leaf to pod, in this veggie fest,
Each one of them thinks they're the best!

Essence of Maturity

There once was a grape, full of cheer,
Whispering jokes to all those near.
"Why so serious, lovely wine?"
It chuckled, 'Ours is a grapevine design!'

With older fruits sharing their tales,
Their wisdom shared through humor prevails.
"Just let yourself ferment, don't resist,
The older you get, the sweeter the twist!"

A prune piped up, "I've seen it all!
Life is a dance, don't be afraid to fall."
Ripe with laughter, they swayed around,
In a jolly twist of laughs they found.

So here's to the fruits, aging with flair,
Finding the joy in every sweet dare.
Essence of years, it's all in good fun,
With each little giggle, they say, we've won!

Fecund Dreams

In the orchard, fruits abound,
But squirrels are dancing all around.
They steal my pears, they grab my figs,
Who knew they'd be such little swigs?

I planted seeds with utmost care,
Hoping for growth, a garden fair.
But weeds declared, 'We're here to stay!'
Now my vegetables just run away!

My bushes bulge with bright delight,
But bees, they buzz, oh what a sight!
They sip and swirl, then take a spin,
In my backyard, it's a wild din!

Harvest time brings all the fuss,
But frogs are jumping all over us.
They ribbit loud, a joyful choir,
As I just try to dodge the mire!

Nature's Melodies in Full Swing

The garden sings in silly tones,
With carrots dancing, claiming thrones.
Tomatoes twirl in shades of red,
While cabbages nod, bumping their heads.

The sun shines bright, it's quite a show,
But ants are marching, oh so slow!
They stop to chat along the way,
As I stand by and yell, 'Hey, hey!'

Butterflies flap, they think they're grand,
While bees make music, strong and planned.
But watch your head, that buzzing critter,
Steals my hat—now isn't that bitter?

Nature's tunes, a comical band,
With fruit flying out like grains of sand.
Some days I laugh, some days I cry,
As veggies plot to make me sigh!

The Tantalizing Wait

Patience is a tricky game,
When you're waiting on the same.
Pumpkins grow, or so I'm told,
Yet all I see is soil so bold.

My salad dreams are fighting hard,
As rabbits plot in my own yard.
They nibble greens, they steal my thyme,
While I just hope—oh c'mon, it's prime!

The longer I wait, the funnier it seems,
Each leaf a tease, or so it deems.
I try a dance to speed the grind,
But all I attract are hungry behinds!

When harvest comes, I'll throw a feast,
Complete with friends, to say the least.
But till that day, I chase my dreams,
While nature giggles, or so it seems!

Overflowing Abundance

My fridge is busting at the seams,
With veggies thrown like flashy dreams.
I've got zucchini, more than I know,
And a squash that could steal the show!

Eggplants jive and beans do sway,
While I try to eat them every day.
But what's the fuss? I'm feeling bold,
When life gives you greens, eat 'til you fold!

The corn is popping—what a spree!
As I embark on a cornucopia spree.
Neighbors peek in, but I don't care,
The party's here—come join my lair!

A bounty in every silly meal,
So here's a toast—let's make a deal.
With laughter loud and spoons in hand,
We'll feast together, just like we planned!

Kissed by the Sun

Beneath a blanket of golden light,
Tomatoes dance in pure delight.
With giggles sprouting from leafy beds,
Even cucumbers wear tiny thread hats.

Carrots chuckle in their orange coats,
While radishes swap silly anecdotes.
The herbs toss jokes like confetti in air,
As bees tune in, buzzing without a care.

The squash tell tales of growing too wide,
While peas play hide-and-seek, full of pride.
And in the patch, with laughter contagious,
All veggies agree: this life is outrageous!

As summer's warmth passes through,
We find joy in all we pursue.
From garden beds to kitchen fun,
We celebrate life, kissed by the sun!

Majestic Harvest

In a field where the giggles sprout,
Corn stands tall, wearing a sprout-patterned clout.
Potatoes share secrets from underground,
While broccoli's wearing a leafy crown.

The pumpkins grumble, 'We feel full and round,'
As gourds spin tales, funny and profound.
The wheat waves gently like a curly-haired friend,
Making sure the fun never ends.

With buckets in hand, we gather the loot,
Zucchini pretending it's really a flute.
As laughter fills the crisp autumn air,
Majesty's found in the joy we share.

Each silly fruit is a treasure we find,
Harvesting smiles, oh how we're aligned!
In this quirky dance of nature's own art,
Every twist, every turn, warms the heart.

Well-Seasoned Whispers

Olive oil whispers tales from a spoon,
While spices giggle, making curry tunes.
Garlic's got jokes, it's not just a clove,
Mixing flavors for a silly stove.

Salt and pepper, a seasoned pair,
Throw in some laughter, that's how we share.
Chili flakes tease with a fiery grin,
As a pot bubbles, let the fun begin!

With veggies in tow, they twist and they spin,
Lettuce takes lead, it's ready to win.
Together they twirl in a culinary dance,
Creating a feast that's pure happenstance.

Well-seasoned whispers, a dinner delight,
Turning mundane meals into pure bite!
So gather your friends, let the fun interlace,
In this kitchen of joy, there's always a place.

Flourishing Growth

In the garden, where giggles unfold,
Seeds burst with stories, eager and bold.
Radishes blush, secrets in tow,
As beans climb up to steal the show.

The daisies dance with their heads held high,
While butterflies flit, oh my, oh my!
Bees do the tango from bud to bloom,
Creating a buzz that fills every room.

The sun in the sky wears a wide silly grin,
Cheering on sprouts as they begin to win.
Joyous growth everywhere you may seek,
In this patch of laughter, we all feel unique.

With every turn in this garden of glee,
Life's lessons are mixed, like honey and tea.
So join in the fun, let the growth be your guide,
In this flourishing haven, let laughter abide!

Wanderlust for Flavor

In the fridge, a mango sits of gold,
Dreams of tropical beaches, bold.
One bite and I'm a travel guide,
Savoring the globe, joy can't hide.

Guacamole whispers from the bowl,
A party in my mouth, it takes a toll.
Avocado dancing, salsa thrives,
Who knew my taste buds had such lives?

Tasting the Lush Life

Pineapple pizza, what a delight,
A culinary dare, I take a bite.
Sweet meets savory, a flavor war,
Did I just open a tasteless door?

Berries tangled in a pancake stack,
A breakfast battle, can't hold back.
The syrup spills like laughter flows,
Shaking my head at how this goes.

Euphoria of the Harvest

Cucumbers grinning like they know,
In my salad, they put on a show.
Tomatoes blush in the summer sun,
Together they frolic, oh what fun!

Oh, corn on the cob, you're a classic,
Chomping down, it's pure elastic.
Butter dripping like a tiny stream,
On my face, a corn-loving dream!

Beneath the Canopy

Mushrooms pop up, like little gnomes,
Playing hide and seek, in forest homes.
With every bite a secret shared,
Nature's jokes—it's unprepared!

Honey dripping like a treasure chest,
Drizzled on toast, I feel so blessed.
Bees buzz around, they're busy fools,
Creating sweetness, bending rules.

Deliciously Awaiting

In the garden, things are peaking,
Tomatoes laugh, the peppers sneaking.
A cucumber slips, it's feeling bold,
While mischievous radishes tell tales of old.

Corn on the cob is plotting a feast,
Whispers of butter, oh what a beast!
The carrots giggle, they're feeling fine,
Hiding beneath, all snug in a line.

Pickles are dancing in a jar,
Salsa's parade isn't too far.
Every veggie's wearing a smile,
Ready for munching in just a while.

Nature's buffet, what a treat!
Mouths are watering, can't be beat.
With joy in hand, we all agree,
Harvesting laughter is the key!

Tapestry of Flavor

Fruits are hanging, wearing their hues,
Bananas boast of their happy views.
Strawberries wink, with seeds in a row,
While apples pretend they're all in the know.

Kiwi jokes with a cheeky grin,
Silly melon dancing, where to begin?
Grapes all gather, holding a feast,
Challenging each other, who's the sweetest beast?

Pineapple juggling all on its head,
Blackberries laughing, 'Let's not be misled!'
Tangerines giggle, all sticky and bright,
Sharing their stories under the moonlight.

All united, oh what a scene,
Gathered in fun, fresh and clean.
In this banquet of laughter, we thrive,
A tapestry of flavor, oh how we arrive!

Essence of Full Bloom

Petals giggle under the sun,
Buds cracking jokes, oh, this is fun!
Sunflowers strut with their heads held high,
While daisies flutter, and the bees buzz by.

Lilies whisper secrets of grace,
Tulips tease with their vibrant embrace.
A rose takes a bow, oh what a flair,
Sharing perfume in the warm spring air.

The daisies argue about who is best,
While pansies laugh and take a rest.
Each bloom a character, bright and wild,
It's a floral party, nature's own child.

In this garden of cheer, all are loud,
Bursting with joy, we're blooming proud.
Life's in full swing, with colors so bright,
Every flower knows how to savor the light!

The Joy of Gathering

In the kitchen, laughter bubbles high,
Chopping and stirring, a cheer-filled sigh.
Friends all gather, with bowls and spoons,
Cooking up mischief, dancing like loons.

Pasta twirls, ready for a dive,
As garlic and herb scents come alive.
The veggies tango, all in a whirl,
While potatoes giggle, it's their turn to swirl.

Toppings fly like a confetti storm,
With each splash and sprinkle, the flavors form.
Laughter erupts as the oven beeps,
Counting down seconds, anticipation leaps.

Together we feast and share a toast,
In this joyful mix, we find our boast.
Because in the warmth of friends and delight,
Every meal's magic, shining so bright!

A Bounty of Whispers

Beneath the tree, a squirrel prances,
Plotting ways to steal my chances.
Fruit hangs low, it calls my name,
But oh! The critter plays a game.

With giggles shared, we share the scene,
He leaps for apples, feeling keen.
I toss a pear, he swings and dives,
In this fruit war, we're both alive!

Where Ages Blossom

Tomatoes flirt on vines so tall,
They blush with joy, I hear their call.
With pranks they play, like jester beans,
Each ripened laugh, a summer's sheen.

Old cucumbers wear wise, wrinkled grins,
They share old tales as laughter spins.
In this garden of giggles and cheer,
The veggies dance, no need for fear!

Fullness of Time

A melon rolled as if to tease,
Chasing shadows, feeling the breeze.
"Catch me if you can!" it shouts,
While zucchinis watch and laugh, in clouts.

In this round race, the pumpkins cheer,
With silly hops, they bring good cheer.
"Just wait till sundown," they say with glee,
"Then we'll be pie and fit for tea!"

The Sweet Approach

Bananas slide off shelves with flair,
"Look at me!" they squeal, "Catch some air!"
As berries bounce with joyful cries,
They form a band 'neath sunny skies.

The peaches blush in cheeky jest,
Organizing a fruit-filled fest.
"Join us now, the fun's begun,
For laughter's sweet and never done!"

Golden Moments in Time

In the fruit bowl, chaos reigns,
A banana wears its spotty stains.
The apples giggle, pear's in a twist,
Feeling so juicy, none can resist.

Grapes are dancing, feeling so fine,
Whispering secrets of sunshine wine.
Orange is blushing, a zestful shout,
Saying, 'Pick me first, without a doubt!'

Pineapple wearing its prickly crown,
Tells all the others, 'I never frown!'
With sweetness ready, it's all a game,
In this golden moment, none feel shame.

So pass the fruit salad, let's all dive,
Life's a banquet, it's fun to thrive!
Every slice brings a chuckle or cheer,
These golden moments are best when near.

Fullness of Life

The fridge is full; a feast awaits,
Bouncing veggies on all the plates.
Carrots in coats, peas in a line,
Cauliflower thinks it's divine!

Tomatoes chuckle, juiciness flows,
While pickles play hopscotch on toes.
Spinach is flexing, feeling so grand,
While lettuce just shrugs, 'I'm taking a stand!'

Cabbage rolls over, don't give a care,
Chasing the garlic, through fragrant air.
In this fullness, funny things bloom,
As we gather and share, fills the room.

Life is a buffet, let's all partake,
With laughter and joy, what's there to fake?
From every dish, let's make a toast,
To the fullness of life, let's cherish the most!

Eager for the Harvest

The garden's buzzing, what's that sound?
Veggies arguing about who's crowned.
Tomato boasts, 'I'm the ripest here!'
While pumpkins bicker, full of cheer.

The corn stands tall, saying, 'I'm elite!'
While radishes blush, feeling the heat.
Zucchini is flexing, showing its size,
But herbs whisper sweetly, sharing their cries.

Baskets are ready, the harvest is near,
As veggies conspire, feeling sincere.
With laughter and fun, they jostle about,
Everyone's eager, ready to sprout.

So come grab a shovel, let's dig and dive,
Into this harvest, we all will thrive.
With funny debates on who shines the best,
The eager ones gather, it's all a jest!

Promised Land of Tastes

In the pantry, treasures galore,
Cereal dances, calling for more.
Chips and salsa throwing a party,
While cookies giggle, feeling so hearty.

Pasta is twirling, sauce on a spree,
Whispering secrets of taste jubilee.
Rice and beans sharing tales of old,
In this promised land, flavors unfold.

Candies prance in bright rainbow hues,
While popcorn pops out, sharing good news.
When every bite brings a smile to the face,
We savor the fun, in this glorious space.

So let's gather round and dig right in,
With laughter as sauce, together we win.
In this promised land where taste takes the lead,
Funny moments blossoming, delicious indeed!

Nature's Generous Heart

In the garden, things are bright,
Tomatoes dancing in the light.
Cucumbers whisper, 'Take a chance!'
While zucchini starts a jolly dance.

Pumpkins laughing, big and round,
In this place, joy can be found.
Beets are blushing, feeling proud,
Cauliflower's hiding in a cloud.

Herbs are giggling in the breeze,
Chasing butterflies with ease.
Lettuce leaves play hide and seek,
In this patch, life's quite unique.

So come and feast, make a plate,
Join the veggies, it's first-rate!
Nature's bounty, such a tease,
A comedy of flavors, if you please.

Quenching the Thirst for Flavor

Juicy oranges in a row,
Squeeze them tight, let goodness flow!
Lemon laughs with citrus cheer,
While lime pretends it's Shakespeare.

Watermelons, big and sweet,
Kicking back like they're on repeat.
With every slice, smiles grow wide,
As fruit plays tricks, matched with pride.

Berries burst with glee so bright,
In bowls they dance, a pure delight.
Strawberries in a spinning show,
Yelling, "Hey! Come join the flow!"

So grab a glass, take a sip,
Join this fruity little trip.
The flavors frolic, what a ride,
In this punchy, tangy tide.

Time to Pluck

In the orchard, fruits hang around,
Pears are grinning, feeling crowned.
Apples shout, "Come take a bite!"
While cherries giggle with delight.

Cutting loose just like a band,
Fruits are swaying, oh so grand!
Plums are winking, saying, "Pick!"
Each fruit's choice is like a trick.

Grapes are clustering, quite unswayed,
Eager to be in the shade.
With beetroot hiding underground,
Joking that it's lost and found.

Gather, gather, make a cheer,
The harvest waits, it's finally here!
With jolts of flavor, zest, and fun,
Grab your basket, this race is won.

The Flavorful Prelude

Let's begin this merry feast,
With colors bright, to say the least.
Celery's marching in a line,
While broccoli's saying, "I'm just fine!"

Peppers juggling, feeling spry,
As onions peek with a shy sigh.
Garlic dances on its toes,
Teasing flavors, see how it flows.

Herbs are plotting in their pots,
Creating mischief with their knots.
Mint is laughing, fresh and bright,
While dill dreams of a culinary night.

So join this party, bring your spoon,
It's a flavor fest, and we're all in tune!
Every bite a little song,
In this lively, nutty throng.

The Tapestry of Yield

In the garden of dreams, fruits hang low,
Tomatoes are blushing, with quite the glow.
Berries in chaos, all jumbled and sweet,
Even the corn seems to tap its own feet.

Pumpkins are rolling, they've lost their own race,
Lettuce is lounging, all up in your space.
Carrots are giggling, they'll dance in the sun,
While onions are crying, yet still having fun.

Zucchinis and eggplants, in a playful ballet,
Just watch them all twirl, come join in the play!
The vines weave a story, so wild and absurd,
Who knew that the harvest could be such a word?

In this patch of delight, we savor each bite,
Living in laughter, from morning till night.
The fruits of our labors, all quirky and free,
A tapestry woven for all to see.

Garden of Possibilities

In a patch of green, where the laughter is loud,
Tomatoes throw parties, so colorful and proud.
Cucumbers gossip, in whispers and grins,
While peppers do salsa, and let the fun begin.

Squash plants are sprawled, like lazy old folks,
Trying to tell all the funniest jokes.
Radishes blush with their shy little flair,
As carrots are scheming to never take care.

With each dawning sun, new hilarity grows,
Broccoli dons costumes, just thought you should know.
They gauge the weather, in a comedic spin,
Forecasting tomorrow's uproar and din.

In the garden of dreams, humor takes flight,
Nature's own circus, a jovial sight.
Harvesting giggles, from soil to the sky,
In this joyful patch, we laugh, oh my!

Lush Moments Awaken

Among the luscious greens, giggles abound,
Grapes in the sun, who weren't shy to be found.
Thyme is up to tricks, with its fragrant delight,
While basil is plotting all day and all night.

Jalapeños sizzle, they think they're on stage,
With carrots as critics, flipping the page.
Beans claim the throne, with a kingly parade,
While corn makes its entrance, with bravado displayed.

Mint's started a band, the herbs in a trance,
As garlic grows bold, and insists on a dance.
In this riotous realm, every laugh's a delight,
Where moments awaken each day and each night.

With baskets of joy, we gather and cheer,
For in this lush chaos, there's nothing to fear.
A banquet of giggles, we find in our quest,
In nature's own bounty, we're truly blessed.

Embrace the Juiciness

In the field's warm embrace, berries start to sing,
Mangoes with giggles, like they've got a fling.
Lemons are teasing, with a zesty old rhyme,
While watermelons roll, losing track of time.

Peaches are blushing, their charm feels like fate,
As apples stand proud, delegating their weight.
Cherries in clusters, they bounce to the beat,
Turning the orchard to a dance on their feet.

Pineapples chuckle, with their spiky crown,
Dancing in sunlight, in nature's own gown.
The flavors collide, in a whimsical stew,
Each berry and fruit, just waiting for you.

In this juice-laden realm, we smile and we share,
With abundance so bright, it just hangs in the air.
Embracing the sweetness, come join in the cheer,
In this playful parade, all fruits disappear!

Bursting with Flavor

In the garden, fruits do dance,
Plump tomatoes in a trance.
Cherries giggle, bounce with glee,
Waving hello to you and me.

Peppers puff up, strutting bold,
Eggplants wear coats of purple gold.
Zucchini jokes with squash nearby,
A vegetable show; oh my, oh my!

Berries blush in rows so neat,
Saying, "Pick us, we're a treat!"
Lemons laugh with zesty cheer,
Telling all, "It's time for beer!"

Fruits in baskets, all a-chatter,
"Open us up; we're not just batter!"
Let's feast together, what a scene!
Harvest of laughter, bright and green!

The Time for Gathering

Gather 'round with baskets wide,
Friends and fam, let's take a ride.
Fields of gold and green await,
Let's be speedy; don't be late!

Corn on the cob, standing tall,
"Pick me, pick me!" they all call.
Pumpkins giggle, orange and round,
"Hey there, buddy! Look what I found!"

Grapes are squeaking, "We're not sour!"
"We're the stars, come taste our power!"
Carrots whisper from the ground,
"Show us the love, let's stick around!"

Let's munch and crunch, enjoy the spree,
Harvesting joy, just you and me.
Nature's cupboard, open wide,
With laughter shared, let's enjoy the ride!

Sun-Kissed Abundance

Oh, the sun, it shines so bright,
Fruits in sunbeams, what a sight!
Peaches blush with giddy glee,
Let's munch a bit, just you and me!

Melons roll with laughter loud,
"Look at us, we're the fruity crowd!"
Grapes in clusters play and hide,
"Come and catch us, it's a fun slide!"

Cucumbers in shades of green,
Whisper secrets, if you lean.
Caramel apples stand in line,
"Try us now; we taste divine!"

Summer's cheer, all around,
Nature's tricks, so profound.
Let's celebrate this juicy trend,
With every bite, let laughter blend!

Nature's Bounty Awaits

Nature's basket, full of cheer,
"Pick us quickly, feast is near!"
Nutty squashes, bright and round,
Taste them all, joy will abound!

Minty herbs with fuzzy leaves,
"Sprinkle us on, before it leaves!"
Sprouts uplift with joyful cries,
"Don't forget us, let's rise and shine!"

Kale gets ruffled, full of sass,
"Who knew veggies could be so brash?"
Radishes roll with little grins,
Making jokes about our sins!

Gather 'round this veggie party,
Dance with relish, oh so hearty.
Nature's bounty, bright and true,
With giggles shared, it's me and you!

Sun-Kissed Futures

Beneath the sun, we laugh and play,
With juicy dreams that make our day.
Bananas dancing, apples twirling,
In the breeze, our hopes are swirling.

Lemons pucker in the light,
Tickling toes, oh what a sight!
Cherries giggle, grapes roll by,
Fruits with jokes that make us sigh.

In this garden, we conspire,
To build our dreams and reach them higher.
Peaches whisper secrets sweet,
While berries bounce upon our feet.

So grab a slice of silly cheer,
For fruity joys are always near.
We'll toss our worries to the sky,
And let our laughter fruitfully fly.

Fruitful Horizons

On the horizon, colors blend,
A playful twist, the fun won't end.
Strawberries wearing silly hats,
Joking with those silly cats.

Mangoes juggle with a frown,
While lemons slide and tumble down.
Oranges giggle, bouncing wide,
In this world, there's no need to hide.

With a twist and a little dance,
Pineapples join our merry chance.
Tropical rhythms fill the air,
As fruits engage in wild affair.

So laugh along, embrace each cheer,
For a fruity life is always clear.
In this silly, fruity race,
We find our joy in every place.

Harvest Moonlight

Under the moon, we dance and sing,
As pumpkins roll and the night takes wing.
Corn cobs wearing goofy grins,
In twilight, where the laughter spins.

Silly shadows in the field,
With each harvest, joy revealed.
Carrots prance with radish flair,
As squashes float up in the air.

The night is ripe for jest and play,
As fruit-friends gather, "Hooray! Hooray!"
In moonlit beams, we join a waltz,
Where veggies tease and share their faults.

So raise a toast to harvest's cheer,
In moony light, our joys appear.
With every wink and leafy joke,
We'll savor life as friendships stoke.

Sweet Fruits of Autumn

Autumn leaves in swirling dance,
Fruits in line for a silly chance.
Apples don their finest shoes,
While pumpkins twirl to share the news.

Cider dreams bubble with delight,
As nuts and berries share the night.
A pear tells jokes to every crowd,
While fritters leave the talk so loud.

Squirrels giggle, gathering treats,
While harvest fun just can't be beat.
A fruit parade upon the street,
With laughter echoing, oh so sweet.

So join the fun as seasons shift,
The world is full of fruity gifts.
In every bite and every laugh,
We cherish life, our sweet aftermath.

www.ingramcontent.com/pod-product-compliance
Lightning Source LLC
Chambersburg PA
CBHW060133230426
43661CB00003B/401